TOUGH
TRUTHS

TOUGH TRUTHS

THE TEN LEADERSHIP LESSONS
WE DON'T TALK ABOUT

DEIRDRE MALONEY

ISBN:
978-0-9840273-2-3 paperback
978-0-9840273-3-0 ebook

Cover and interior design by *the*BookDesigners, www.bookdesigners.com

Printed in the United States of America

First Printing

**Business
Solutions
Press**
113 West G Street, #647
San Diego, CA 92101
(619) 209-7749
www.makemomentum.com

Publisher's Cataloging-In-Publication Data
(Prepared by The Donohue Group, Inc.)

Maloney, Deirdre.
Tough truths : the ten leadership lessons we don't talk about / Deirdre Maloney.

   p. ; cm.

   Issued also as an ebook.
   ISBN: 978-0-9840273-2-3 (pbk.)

   1. Leadership. 2. Success in business. I. Title.

HD57.7 .M35 2012
658.4/092

DEDICATION

To my extraordinary mother,

Patricia Costa,

who proves that great leadership comes with
authentic relationships, boundless energy
and only the highest level of class.

CONTENTS

INTRODUCTION
The Truth About This Book

Welcome.

If you've cracked open this book you're hoping to learn something new about leadership.

I'm glad to have you. Though I must tell you, there's a chance you might not like everything I have to say. In fact, some of the lessons might sting a bit. You might resist them, tell yourself this just *can't* be the way it is.

I understand. I've done it, too.

What I'd like to personally ask is that you spend our brief bit of time together with an open mind, that you allow yourself to just acknowledge that – like it or not – these lessons might be true.

Some of them came by way of my own leadership journey (which isn't even close to complete). Others came from the journeys of others.

I didn't learn these lessons through a big research project. I wasn't grant funded for a longitudinal study. Instead, I just paid a lot of attention. I paid attention to people I consider to be great leaders and learned what to do. I paid attention to people who seem to miss the mark and learned what to avoid.

This book was born out of a series of my blog posts. They all focus on a nugget of truth about leadership, a nugget that often makes us uncomfortable. After all, as we all know, sometimes the truth is tough.

Over time my blogs have gotten a bit of a reputation for being a bit – shall we say – forthcoming. At one point a loyal follower contacted me and asked me to speak on some of his favorite posts for his company. I would be speaking at a special awards luncheon, filled with employees recognized for their own outstanding leadership. He wanted me to inspire them, to teach them how to enhance their own skills. He wanted me to say it differently.

So I pulled together my favorite blogs and made this list.

Here's how I knew the truths hit home.

The awards luncheon was delightful. It was held at an amazing restaurant in town, one known for its delicious cuisine and decadent desserts. My speech came just as that decadence was being served in all its glory.

As I introduced the *Tough Truths* topic I could tell the audience was intrigued. And by the time I got to lesson #3 or so I realized something funny. Nobody had touched their Crème Brulee, nor their Chocolate Ganache. They were all just…listening. Forks down. Eyes up.

I admit even I was surprised. After all, I knew this group was into leadership…but really? It was *Crème Brulee* for goodness' sake!

That's when I knew how much people would appreciate these tough truths. That's when I knew how it important it was to spread them around.

I believe that the path to great leadership is like a chess game, and I love watching great leaders play it.

Great leaders know that every step they take, every decision they make, matters in the end. They know they must strategize carefully, then act aggressively. They know they must think ahead – not just to their next step – but to the many steps after it. They know they must always be on the look-out for opportunities, and for others who will fight them for the same.

The difference between the pawn and the king (or the queen, by the way) is that the pawn is not flexible. The king is willing to move in any direction at any time. The king understands when to push forward, and when to stand still, strong and tall.

There's a reason there is just one king and one queen on each side of the board. Because it's tough to become one. Because it's scary to take risks. Because it takes a combination of savvy, smarts and heart to win the game in the end.

Yet, hard as this game might be, the king and the queen are the ones we pay the most attention to. They are the ones we watch the most closely, the ones whose moves we anticipate with curiosity, delight, and envy. They are the ones who ultimately make the difference between a win and a loss.

The truth is we are all part of the leadership game. It's just up to us to figure out which role we're willing to play.

Which is what this book is all about.

One word of warning before you begin.

As you pick a few favorite lessons and begin to practice them, you might find that things are a bit less comfortable in your own work environment. Just because you are becoming an even better leader doesn't mean those around you are doing the same. All of a sudden you might find you are a bit out of sync with others in your office or the powers that be.

Just know this is natural, that extending out of your comfort zone is a healthy and strong choice. In my book, *The Mission Myth*, I write about the importance of redefining success. In this case, even though things might get awkward, even though they might be a little less enjoyable, I encourage you to celebrate your success - the fact that you are growing, even if those around you aren't. The fact that you won't let it stand in your way. It might not feel like a success, but I assure you it is.

Yes, it might make things a bit tricky. You might even decide to find something that fits you better in the long run. And while change is hard, this might just be the best decision you could make.

A final word on these lessons.

I'm not going to pretend for even a second that I've mastered all of them. In fact, I've mastered none of them.

Instead, I work on them every day. I keep them in mind as I go about my daily life, engage with people, consider my goals.

I practice them. I say them to myself over and over. And when I come up short, I allow myself to remember that this is a work in progress...that I am a work in progress.

That I am a great leader in progress.

For those who are already there, I congratulate you. And I thank you for teaching me these tough truths.

Because, in the end, I know they'll make all the difference.

In what I can do in this world.

And how happy I am in it.

For those of you in progress as well, I'm glad to have you here with me.

Enjoy the journey.

LEADERSHIP LESSON #1
The Truth About Your Politics

I begin with a lesson that might fill you with disdain. It's one where I tend to get some push-back. Many truly believe they can just rise above it, ignore it, and be a great leader anyway.

Wrong.

Here's what great leaders know about politics…

TRUTH #1
Politics are Everywhere

To be clear, by politics I'm not talking about the pundits we see daily on our various media, vying for our votes and our money.

What I'm talking about are the politics you and I are involved in everyday, simply because we interact with people who have what we want, and who want what we have to give.

I found my favorite definition of politics on a generic website, but it serves my point well. Politics is "the aggregate of relationships of people in society." It is how we come together as people in various ways each day, how we hold conversations and – sometimes without even knowing it – work those relationships to get something out of life.

The most controversial part of all? This is not a *bad* thing. This is the way the world – and we as a people – work. Whether we want our boss to give us a raise, our child to stop squirming on the airplane, or the department store to take back our purchase when we don't have a receipt, every single interaction involves influencing and persuading others in order to get what we want.

Often times what we want is simply a warm friendship or some loving support. It might not feel like politics because it's so authentic, because it comes so easily, because it doesn't require any kind of traditional *politicking*.

But think of it this way. These relationships are valuable to us – perhaps more valuable than anything – and we want to keep them. And so we honor the other person by giving back, checking in, sending thank-you notes. We know that these things mean something to them and so we want to make them feel good. In the end, even that gives us something. We get to feel better about ourselves.

Great leaders understand that politics are everywhere, that a great work ethic alone will not get them as far as a great work ethic and the ability to have relatable, effective and influential relationships.

They understand this, then embrace it. They utilize it every day. They know that, even if a relationship doesn't produce something right now, it may eventually. They never let their guard down on their interactions - big or small, fleeting or ongoing - because they know relationships are gold.

Gold.

That's why they get ahead, while the rest of us wonder why the guy in the cubicle next to us just got promoted when we're the ones working our butts off until 9pm every night.

A brief example…

Let's get this out of the way early. There's something you should know about me.

When I'm not writing or preaching about leadership lessons, I'm a body-builder. A fairly committed one. We'll get to the reason why later, but for now let me just say that I'm known for being a bit…obsessive.

Because it's a pretty long routine and because I like to get in and out of there as quickly as possible to start the rest of my day, I show up before the gym even opens at 5am.

Yes, I'm one of *those*, standing outside the front door when the poor 20-somethings show up, the night-sky still very much inky-black. All they want to do is unlock the door, take a sip of coffee and get their game face on before greeting the mass of adrenaline junkies.

Yet there I am, hoping to be let in early so that I can get started. Hoping, let's face it, for special treatment. For them to let me in behind them, allow me to sneak up the stairs to the equipment before anyone else.

It used to be that I wasn't all that engaging during this process. After all, I was tired myself. I didn't feel like it mattered if I stayed quiet or chatted away. And what did these 20-somethings care about my eager-beaver dedication anyway?

But then I noticed something.

In the beginning, when I stood there with my arms crossed and just asked to follow them into the gym before the appointed open time, they would shake their heads and point out the management policy. Not allowed.

Then…I tried being nicer, more pleasant. It wasn't that I was fake. I didn't turn into some kind of annoyingly chipper workout fiend. Instead I just started asking how they were doing as they unlocked the door. I gave them some room to complain, told them I couldn't imagine having to get up so early and give good customer service. I thanked them – by name - when they let me in. I thanked them – by name - on the way out. I was real, but I also understood that these people had something I wanted. And if I wanted to get it, I had to work the relationship.

Soon, four out of five of them let me in behind them. Because they liked me better. Because I was more *likeable*.

And here's the bonus. I actually found that by being more pleasant to them, I felt more pleasant inside. Turns out that giving these unsuspecting gatekeepers a tiny bit of energy raised my own.

That fifth guy? I'm still working on him. But no matter what he'll never see my arms crossed in front of me.

In the end, I know that will never get me anywhere.

Today…

Take notice of every interaction you have. Notice how differently things happen when you go out of your way to be even more pleasant, when you smile from the start, thank people more than once. It doesn't take much, but in the long run you'll get more of what you want.

Which will make you more successful. Which will get you a happier life.

LEADERSHIP LESSON #2
The Truth About What Others Think of You

Next up is a leadership lesson that even some of the greatest leaders don't know in the beginning.

It doesn't occur to them until they actually get into their leadership roles and begin to find success. And then it hits them square in the face.

All of a sudden they look around and realize the truth about great leaders…

TRUTH #2
Great Leaders Aren't Liked Very Much

It stings, I know. And let me be clear that yes, some people *do* like great leaders, stand by them through every hill and valley. Others? They just don't. And a few downright hate them.

It's a harsh reality. We take on leadership roles because we believe we can make a difference, make things better. Whether it's an upper management position, a mid-level supervisor or a board role, we think we've got what it takes to make it sing, that we'll be the ones to rally our teams, make our organizations better than they were before. Along the way we will energize the masses, get them to buy into our strategies, celebrate our successes.

It's a grand idea. And, for most of us, a fantasy.

Here's what really happens.

We get into a leadership role and, at first, we're celebrated. Our bosses and our staff pull for us. They watch us carefully as we delve into our new position, as we interact with others, as we speak of the many achievements we'll conduct in this great company-wide orchestra.

Then we actually begin to achieve those things, and we realize those wins, the ones we were so excited about, come with a price. They make us unpopular. They make us less liked.

What happened? Well, we did just what we said we were going to. We found success. Which means we made changes, held people accountable and moved forward with purpose and determination.

Change freaks people out. It makes people mad. So do performance evaluations, which great leaders often need to do. So do decisions that come without complete consensus, which great leaders often need to make.

And so those same people who were pulling for us now talk about us to each other, to anyone who will listen. They say we are making things worse, that we are no better than the last one, that we don't *get it*.

I say again, some do continue to support us, but many others fall away. And all of a sudden we realize that we need to come to work with more than a smiling face. We need a strong will and an even stronger stomach. Because somewhere along the way the masses stopped rallying around us. And we find ourselves alone.

Great leaders know that when they do what they need to do to get results, they simply won't be liked very much by some people. They sacrifice being liked in order to focus on achieving concrete goals, making hard decisions, creating change.

Even when those changes are made in the most supportive way, where staff gets to give all kinds of input beforehand, they know it won't necessarily matter.

Unless they find the magical way to make every single person happy with every single decision they make, their likeability quotient will inevitably go way down.

What makes these leaders great is this: even though they aren't liked by many, even though they're hated by some, even though they find themselves alone, they do the hard stuff anyway.

Because in the end they know their ultimate success isn't about how many people think they're great.

It's about whether or not their organizations are.

A brief example…

I was promoted into an executive position, running a multi-million dollar nonprofit organization, at the tender age of 28.

I'd come up from within the ranks and thought things would be perfect, that my loyal colleagues and friendly co-workers would stand by my side. That, together, we'd make the organization soar.

Here's how I figured out the fantasy.

Before the promotion I had lunch with my colleagues regularly. Each day we'd get together and sign out for an hour as we pondered our cuisine of choice, then walked over to our venue du jour, laughing together and swapping stories about work and life.

One month after my promotion – after I'd made my first set of vacation policy changes and let my first person go - I walked by the lobby at about noon and realized how empty it was. I looked at the sign-out sheet and there were the names of the colleagues with whom I'd always lunched and munched and laughed.

The names were all signed out...but one. Mine. I shrugged away the sting as I wondered why they didn't include me.

And then I realized the harsh truth.

They didn't want me there.

It was tough to swallow, but even on that very first day I knew why it had happened. I knew that – even though it felt exactly the opposite – it really wasn't personal.

I knew that, in the end, I couldn't let it matter. In fact, it was better this way.

I wasn't hired to be liked. I was hired to do right by my organization.

It just meant I had to find new friends. Outside the office.

Far outside.

(For the whole story on this tumultuous part of my professional journey, check out my book *The Mission Myth*.)

Today...

Think about the greatest leaders you know – not the ones you *like* best necessarily – but the ones who have been truly effective. The ones who have made real, positive change.

Next time you see them you might crack a smile at them. Trust me, it could go far. Because you're probably one of the few who will do it.

And if you're one of those great, lonely leaders, take heart. You're not alone.

It just feels like you are.

LEADERSHIP LESSON #3
The Truth About Your Stories

This next lesson might also be a bit painful to hear. But trust me, it'll be worth it.

I begin by again asking you to think about the great leaders you know, the ones who can walk into any room and engage any person about anything.

Words seem to come easily, laughs even easier.

These people have the uncanny ability to make every person they speak to feel special, as if they are the only person in the room. As if they are important.

These people are also just…interesting. They get people's attention, they make people want to engage, to *stay* engaged.

They have a gift, it seems. And oh, how we envy them!

These great leaders know the secret. They know how to get people on their side, how to get someone to like them. And despite what it might seem when you sit there and observe their fluid, easy conversations, it's not about how they talk. It's about what they say.

Or, more to the point, what they don't.

These leaders know the reality of the situation. As much as they think their own lives are fascinating, as much as they love their own tales about their kids, their stories about their latest fantasy football win, their juicy saga about the boss who just got fired, they know the truth...

TRUTH #3
Nobody Will Find You as Interesting as You Do

Sure, others might be mildly interested in what you have to say, but they don't want it to go on forever. They don't even want it to go on longer than just a few minutes. Maybe less. Think of the conversations you like best. Are they filled with long stories? With tedious details? With redundant points and lots of examples you don't care about?

I didn't think so. And great leaders know it. So they do two things.

First...

They say just enough to be interesting, and then they stop. Every time and everywhere.

They keep their stories short, their complaints even shorter. They don't send long emails nor memos that go on for pages. They leave the other person wanting more.

Then...

They get the focus off of them and on to the other guy. And that's truly when the magic happens.

They get the other guy talking about *his* life, about *his* dreams, about *his* kids and *his* boss. They do it because they know that, when people share more, they trust more. And that's how you get one level deeper. Which is what it's all about.

How do they do it? They ask great questions.

Their questions might start with "what do you do?", but they don't stay that simple that long.

- If the guy says he's a lawyer they ask if he ever gets to litigate, and what that's like.

- If the woman says she's a chef they find out if she's into pastry, and ask how in the heck she gets her crusts so flaky without burning them.

- If the guy is into watching baseball they ask about his favorite players, and what makes them so special.

They show that they're interested in more than the topic, in more than polite conversation.

They are interested in the *other guy*. And they are authentic about it all. Because they know they'll not just get one level deeper, but they also might learn something along the way.

Oh, and during these conversations they also keep their phones tucked away, get the person's name right, and never, ever let their eyes wander around the room to see who they might talk to next.

A *brief example…*

I learned this lesson from an absolute master of engagement.

He was a colleague of my husband's at the time, and a group of us attended a baseball game together. Right from the start he began asking me questions.

He asked me about my job, about why I chose it, about how I got there. He asked me how I liked supervising people, and the tricks I'd learned along the way.

He asked me about my family, about what it's like to be the youngest sibling.

He asked me about my love for poker, and whether I was in it to win it or just in it for fun. And why.

Hours passed, and by the time we hit the seventh inning stretch I realized I hadn't shut up.

I also realized that I felt incredibly special and interesting.

And I really liked this guy.

Why? Because he *made me feel* special and interesting. Because he seemed genuinely into what I had to say. Because, now that I'd shared all that information with him, I trusted him more.

The best part is the ending to this story. Shortly after my interaction with him I found out this guy had left my husband's company for the perfect job. He went to work for the FBI, where he would be asking all kinds of people all kinds of things.

No lie.

Today...

Embrace the truth. Nobody will care about your life as much as you do.

Keep your emails short and your stories shorter.

Resist the temptation to go on and on about your morning stuck in traffic and ask the other guy great questions instead. Practice engaging someone new by getting the focus off of you.

Watch what happens. Chances are you'll be a level deeper in no time.

LEADERSHIP LESSON #4
The Truth About Your Fear

After reading the first third of this book you might be feeling a bit overwhelmed – by the politics, by the loneliness. By the fact that others might not find you as interesting as you thought they did.

I understand.

And that's why this next lesson has landed in this spot. Because it's one that will lighten the air a bit, perhaps give you a zap of energy.

But in order for that to happen you need to believe it. Which you might not do at first. I ask that you try anyway.

I begin with what we all believe to be true about great leaders. At least at first.

We talked in the last lesson about our observations of great leaders...how we watch them achieve great things, work a room, get things done with seem-ing ease. How we envy them.

We believe that their success is due to the fact that they are so certain that they will win, that they are so fearless, that they just make it happen.

The truth? It's exactly the opposite.

So here it is. My gift to you. Listen closely...

TRUTH #4

*Every Single Person,
Even the Greatest Leader
Out There, is Afraid*

No matter who they are, no matter what they say to you, no matter what you believe about them, they are all afraid.

Just like the rest of us.

We *are* all afraid, aren't we? Think about it.

We are afraid of failing. We are afraid of screwing up. We are afraid of looking stupid.

Great leaders are, too.

How do I know?

I've been surrounded by some of the most successful, professional, self-assured people around. I make it my job to get to know them - what makes them successful, what makes them tick. Each time I've convinced myself that this is the one, the one who isn't afraid of anything.

But then, when I've truly gotten to know these people, truly understood them, I've learned that they are just as afraid as the rest of us.

Who in the world wants to fail? Who wants to make a fool of themselves? Who wants to be known as the guy who screwed things up?

Yet we refuse to believe it.

We allow ourselves to believe that, not just great leaders, but every single person we come across, is so together, so confident. We allow ourselves to believe they are so strong *because* they aren't afraid of anything.

That their lack of fear is what sets them apart.

Wrong. It is not their lack of fear that sets them apart.

What sets them apart is that they are afraid and *act anyway*.

As much as great leaders would love to live the rest of their lives not looking stupid or failing or being hated, they are more afraid of hiding away and getting nothing done.

They know that true success, true innovation, means trying new things, making hard choices, taking calculated risks.

They know that, as a result, sometimes they *will* fail. They *will* look stupid. But that it will be short lived. And in the meantime they will have learned and grown. They will do better next time. And, in the end, they will get further.

Great leaders are afraid. And they admit it. And they act anyway.

To be clear, it isn't easy for them either. They struggle and they doubt. But in the end, they almost always act. Because the fear of what happens if they don't is far, far worse.

They also believe they can take a risk because even if they fail, they'll fix it. Even if they look stupid, they aren't. Even if they appear weak, they're not.

They know they can deal with whatever consequences come their way. Even though they really, really hope they won't have to.

Ironically, it's those leaders who swear they aren't afraid of anything, the ones who proudly prance around and let everyone know just how successful they are, who are the most afraid of all.

They just won't admit it. To you. To themselves.

A brief example…

I had the chance to work with a major foundation executive from New York a few years ago.

I'd known about him for quite some time. He was legendary, known as a great leader - one who is effective and tough, but also personable and likeable. He was known for taking big risks, giving big grants, making big decisions.

Always a sucker for great leaders, and always wanting to learn everything I can about them, I engaged him one-on-one immediately (see Leadership Lesson #3 for how I did it).

By the end of the very first day, here's what I found out.

• He's afraid of spending the foundation's money in a way that doesn't honor the wishes of the founder.

• He's afraid that his lack of experience in the non-profit world will cause him to make a mistake that hurts the organization.

• He's afraid that he'll let something slip through the cracks, something vitally important.

But, here's the rest of the story.

• He makes the grants anyway, because he's got a good process and knows he's doing it with the best of intentions.

• He leads the organization anyway, because he knows that the non-profits are counting on him to do so.

• He keeps great lists and knows that whatever might slip through the cracks can be fixed.

He acts anyway.

What makes him a great leader isn't his fear. What makes him a great leader is that he's self-assured enough to know that, even if his greatest fears come true, his organization will make it through. And so will he.

Today...

Pay attention to the great leaders you know. Know that they are afraid. Watch how they act anyway.

Be inspired to do the same.

LEADERSHIP LESSON #5
The Truth About The Guy Next to You

Next up... a lesson that might strike you as a bit creepy. Stay with me.

One of the things you can always count on from great leaders is that they are cool under pressure. Really, they're just cool everywhere.

They never, ever let their guard down.

No matter what they're dealing with, no matter who they're talking to, no matter where they are, great leaders present a self-assured, friendly, confident persona.

Why do they do it?

Because they know this next truth...

TRUTH #5
Someone is Always Watching

Bad things happen. We get stressed. We get stuck in major traffic on the way to an important meeting. We have a fight with our spouse right before a client presentation. We get bad news just as the evening's networking function gets underway.

We are tempted to let it show on our faces. We give ourselves permission to shut our office door a little harder, to ignore our staff as they sit in the lunchroom, to bust through the lobby of our office without acknowledging anyone.

We think it won't matter. That nobody is paying attention anyway.

I assure you it matters. Because someone is always watching. They will pay attention to what you are doing and saying. Even if you're acting differently because of a bad day. Actually, especially then. Because you're making a spectacle of yourself. Because you're giving them something to focus on. Someone sitting next to you at a meeting will notice your heavy sighs. Someone in the same audience at a workshop will notice your constant fidgeting. Someone at the table next to you at lunch will notice if your eyes are constantly rolling, your arms are crossed defensively in front of you, your hair is askew from running your hands through it.

People watch. People talk. And communities are small.

Whether you know them or not, people are watching. And one day you might need them.

Great leaders know this. That's why they get it together before every interaction. They never let their guard down. They never let you see them sweat.

They know that it takes a lifetime to build a great reputation, but an instant to flush it all away.

And it could happen because of someone you don't even know is there.

Now, I do know that we all need to whine now and again. We do need to let off steam with a few trusted people so that we can hold it together when we get in front of everyone else.

I absolutely agree. The trick, of course, is figuring out exactly who these *few trusted people* are. The ones we can trust. The ones who are rooting for us. The ones who will help us move forward.

In *The Mission Myth* I write about how to put together your SWAT team, which is the small (smaller than you might be thinking) group of people you give yourself permission to kvetch to. These are the excellent people who help you through. They are your champions. They are special.

Know who is and – perhaps more importantly – is *not* a SWAT team member. Then let those who make it in know you need them for support, and let them know that this very critical role means you might need to let your guard down with them every once in a while.

Just choose carefully so you can truly allow yourself the space and time to get your frustrations out of your system.

And make sure nobody else is around when you do.

A brief example...

I was meeting with a colleague about a project in the lobby of an office building.

Out of nowhere things turned heated. I'm still not quite sure what happened, but all of a sudden this person's voice rose a bit, his tone turned angry and he accused me of ignoring his point of view.

I was taken aback and felt my own temperature rise, but I also knew two things.

First, I needed to not respond in the moment. I needed to let myself cool down and address his tone later, after I'd had some time to think through my message. Otherwise, I might say something I'd regret.

And so I forced myself to keep an even tone, to keep my non-verbals to myself. As calmly as I could I expressed my opinion, apologized for the misunderstanding, and kept my language professional. The second thing I knew was that I needed to end the conversation before things took a turn for the worse. So I did.

Several hours later I was sitting next to a woman in the break room. I'd never seen her before, but it didn't take long for me to realize she was an accomplished, influential person in town – someone I wanted on my side and in my contact list. We were chatting enough that I'd gotten a level deeper (see Leadership Lesson #3). Toward the end she turned to me and said…

"You know, I don't want you to think I was listening in on your conversation, but I have to tell you something. I happened to be working on my computer right next to you in the lobby this morning. I don't know who that person was, but he was sure laying into you. And I have to say, you really kept it together the whole time."

Random, yes? But I swear it's tr ue.

Even better? I've since gotten to know her well and she is now a trusted colleague, one firmly planted in my contact list. Our professional relationship is one of authentic, mutual respect.

It was all because this woman liked what she saw back on that very first day we met…when I didn't know anybody was watching.

Today…

First, don't be freaked out. This lesson is about what makes us human, our need to observe what's happening around us.

Second, notice who is in your midst. And know that they notice you, too.

Third, every time you say or do anything today, think about whether or not you'd be okay if it was passed on to others. Then act accordingly.

LEADERSHIP LESSON #6
The Truth About Your Energy

We all know that great leaders know how to use everything they've got to get ahead.

They know how to manage their time and get things done efficiently. They know how to spend well, to get the biggest proverbial bang for their biggest proverbial buck.

They know how to use their skills with the right people in the right ways to get the best possible outcomes.

There's another asset these leaders know how to spend wisely, and it's one we don't think about.

Really, for most of us, it's not even on the radar. Until we run out. And then we're in all kinds of trouble.

It's the subject of our next truth…

TRUTH #6
Great Leaders Diligently Protect Their Energy

Every single one of us is involved in certain things that give us energy and others that just suck it right out of us. Certain jobs, certain tasks, certain *people* all have this impact on us.

Most of the time we take on our day without anticipating which pieces and people will do what to our energy. We schedule our time randomly – almost haphazardly – plugging tasks and people into our calendars like a geometric puzzle instead of setting ourselves up for success.

Often times we'll take on a task – even volunteer for one – that seems easy enough, even though it involves a project we know we hate or a person who we know will get under our skin.

Then we get to the end of the day and wonder why we're not just tired, but depleted. Fatigued. Cranky.

It's all about the energy. And it's pretty simple in concept.

Great leaders know what gives them energy and they increase it. They know what takes it away and they decrease it.

They know the people who boost them up and so they seek them out, see them more. They know those who leave them feeling exhausted and so they plan for their time together strategically.

The simple formula:

More energy = more often.

Less energy = less often.

As simple as these eight words seem, we disregard them, ignore them. We allow ourselves to believe we are trapped in a world where we just have to do certain things with certain people at certain times.

And that's true. Sometimes. But not nearly as frequently as we think it is.

We have a say in the tasks we take on in the mornings versus the afternoons. We know which ones we need more energy for and we know when we are at our best. We can plan accordingly.

We have a say in who we meet for meals, networking, or activities. We know who fills us with energy and who requires more focus and discipline. We can plan accordingly.

We have a say in our jobs. We have a say in our volunteer roles. We have a say in what we eat, what time we go to bed, what kind of television we watch.

Yes, television.

Me? I take my TV seriously. In fact, and I'm not afraid to admit this, I take my *reality* TV seriously. I've been known to take delight as people abandoned on a desert island engage in psychological warfare on each other. I enjoy watching chefs battle it out over squirming eels. I might find myself watching aspiring singers try to make their way to the top of the musical heap.

But, believe it or not, I do draw the line. I stop at any reality TV where people scream at each other. I don't watch women claw at each other and I can't take it when couples scream at each other…strictly to become famous for *something*.

While the shallow dialogue and high-pitched yells might make me feel better about myself, it's not the energy I want to carry with me. And in the end, I know this isn't necessarily about what I like best or least, but what's best for my energy. The two aren't always the same.

Yes, you have to meet with your boss at certain times. You have to sync with other people's schedules. You have to do your taxes by the middle of April.

But.

The rest of it – really – is up to you.

So figure out what gives you energy and what takes it away. And plan accordingly.

Decrease the things and people that suck the life out of you.

I promise, you have a say in this.

Increase the things and people that fill you up.

I promise, you have a say in this.

A brief example...

Back when I lived in Denver I sat on the board of my homeowner's association.

Now, anyone that's sat on an HOA board knows that they can get pretty dysfunctional. For some reason, when you bring people together and make decisions about their greatest assets – their homes – they turn a bit nutty. Decisions about which landscaping firm to use and which shade of green will work for the new fence become matters of life and death. Things turn personal, dramatic, sometimes nasty.

I found myself dreading the meetings. I hated the drama, and didn't really care about most of the discussion. Even worse, the meetings were held at 7am, a time reserved for my own morning routine (see Leadership Lesson #1).

I allowed myself to believe I was trapped. After all, I'd made a two-year commitment. And I simply didn't go back on my commitments.

One morning I found myself whining (again) about it to a close friend over breakfast. The monthly meeting was just days away, and a controversial "pool cleaner" discussion promised to make it especially unpleasant. It would be terrible, would suck my energy dry.

After several minutes of hearing me out she finally turned to me and asked, "so, why torture yourself? Why don't you just quit?"

I paused, my fork in the air. "Because my neighbors are counting on me," I said, my own martyr tone making me cringe the second it came out.

"No they're not," she said. "If they cared that much, they'd be on the board. You clearly hate it. And it's terrible for your energy. You don't need to do this."

I put my fork down. She was right. I had a choice. This board was no fun. Things change. Commitments can be broken. And this commitment took away critical energy, energy I needed for other projects. It took time away from my workouts, from my husband, from *me*. Even when the meetings were over, the resulting lost energy and cranky mood lasted for hours. Sometimes days.

And so I made my choice. I quit. I got my power back. I got my energy back.

I was better for it.

And I've never had one moment of regret.

Today...

Think about your energy. It's not just about what you like best (like junky reality TV), but about what feeds you, and what depletes you. And who.

Do what you can to increase the good stuff and decrease the bad.

Do what you can to schedule your day accordingly.

Yes, it's easier said than done. But that doesn't mean you can't do it.

You just need to realize you have the power to do so. Much more than you may have thought.

Do it...and be better at what you do.

INTERMISSION

Well, hello there! Welcome to intermission.

Why this seemingly random break in the middle of a book, you ask? In the middle of a *mini-book* nonetheless?

Because I firmly believe this book lives up to its name, that in just the last six chapters you have experienced some tough, tough truths. If the last lesson taught me anything it's that energy matters, and as a result of all this toughness, yours might have taken a dip.

I understand.

What I want *you* to understand clearly is that these lessons are tough for pretty much everyone. Few do them perfectly. Even fewer do them perfectly every time. If they weren't tough, we'd have great leaders everywhere. We wouldn't have to read books about how to be great because it would be so obvious, so easy.

And that's clearly not the case.

And so I built this break in to remind you of a few things.

First of all, you're doing great just by getting this far. Others will have closed the book by now, denied every single lesson. But not you! You're open to embracing new ideas. Which puts you ahead of the game.

Second, as daunting as it might seem so far, there are things you can do right away – small things – that will up your greatness immediately. Just pay attention to the *Today* tips at the end of each chapter and pick your favorites.

Third, take heart…you're more than halfway there!

Finally, if you need a break, you hereby have my explicit permission to take one.

Take a walk. Take a nap. Whatever works for you.

Just promise me you'll come back.

Because there's more to share. And these next lessons are good.

I can't promise they're any easier. But I can promise they'll increase your level of greatness even more.

See you in a few.

LEADERSHIP LESSON #7
The Truth About How You Feel About Yourself

You know what I love about great leaders? The truly great ones?

They have no need to tell you how great they are.

These leaders possess an incredible, unique trait. It doesn't seem all that special when you first hear about it, but it's rare. Very rare.

This special trait is our next truth…

TRUTH #7
Great Leaders Possess Supreme, Undying Confidence

Great leaders know that they are good at what they do. They know they can get things done. They know that if they don't know how to get something done, they'll figure it out. Because they're smart. Because they've done it before.

And because they know this about themselves, they don't need to constantly surround themselves with people who puff them up. And they don't take it personally when others put them down (or, if they do, they refuse to hold onto it).

Sure, they know how to stand up for themselves. But for the most part they know that being a great leader means they won't be liked by everyone (see Leadership Lesson #2).

And so they keep the boasting to a minimum and they don't take it personally when others talk about them behind their backs. They let it go.

Instead they focus on getting things done. And when they do and people notice, they don't take the credit, choosing instead to spread it to their staff, boards, volunteers and the community. They're the ones who shrug off compliments. They're the ones who take the hit when things don't go well.

They do this because they're confident, so they don't need others to tell them how great they are. And they certainly don't need to tell it to others.

Because they're secure enough to know the part they've played in every success.

Because the only glory they'll ever need is knowing they've gotten things done.

And, even though achieving absolute, 100% confidence at every turn is something most people will never do, great leaders are confident enough to know that in the end, no matter what, they will find success. And so they move forward with their heads held high, with a seeming impenetrable sense of security.

Now, the million dollar question.

Just how do the rest of us get some of this confidence?

First, we figure out where our insecurities lie and we deal with them on our own. (Therapy and/ or a good financial planner might be involved. I've engaged with both.)

Then, once we're square with ourselves, once we recognize the qualities and skills we bring to every table, we let the results do the talking for us. We celebrate our wins, but quietly.

And, when others talk about us, gossip about us, try to sabotage us, we put it in perspective. We know that this is what comes with being a great leader. And then we go home, find the people that give us energy (see Leadership Lesson #6), deal with it, and get ready for another day.

A *brief example...*

One of my best bosses ever was at one of my first jobs ever – scooping ice cream at a family restaurant.

What made him so great?

Well, he was charming. He would gather us around and talk about how we were going to break all the records around customer service, that we would exceed expectations. He would talk about his vision, get us to join him, make us laugh. He would compliment the staff – in public - when he saw us doing something right.

But.

There were times when the charm wore off. He would change up our schedules so that we had to work late one night and then early the next morning. He would switch around the wait staff so that they had to juggle tables in different areas of the restaurant. He would call us back to work the very minute our dinner break was up. He had his reasons for all of it, no doubt, and would sometimes even try to explain them. But we didn't care enough to listen.

Those were the times when we didn't find his smile so bright. Those were the times when we would duck in the supply closet and complain, saying he didn't care, that he was messing with us for no reason.

He knew we did it, of course. If it got to him, he never let it show. He was secure enough to know he was doing what needed to be done to meet the company's goals, and that was the most important thing.

Because in the end, he did. Our store was consistently noted as one of the highest performers in the country. We were seen as a model for others. And when people would celebrate him for it, he'd smile quietly, then praise the staff and thank the customers. After all, he'd say, we were all the real reasons behind the success.

In the end, he didn't last all that long at our store.

He was promoted all the way to the top.

Today...

Understand where your insecurities lie. Know that if you have to explain yourself constantly, take lots of credit, or refrain from risk, then you're not coming off as a top leader.

And know there might just be something about your level of self-confidence that you need to work out.

Then work it out. Know you're great. And let the results you get show it to everyone else.

LEADERSHIP LESSON #8
The Truth About Your Reputation

This next lesson is another toughie.

It's not tough in concept, but it tests us in practice. It tests us each and every day, often many, many times each day. Many, many of us fail.

And it hurts us.

It all leads directly to our next truth…

TRUTH #8
*Great Leaders Never,
Ever Talk Trash*

We fail in this lesson each time we speak negatively about our organization or the people in it...or our favorite book group or its leader. Or the friend of a friend.

The trash can be tiny – a simple rolling of the eyes when a person's name comes up. Or it can be landfill-sized, like sitting with people we kind of know at a networking event and telling them that we suspect our boss is having an affair.

It doesn't matter.

Great leaders know that talking trash – big or small, often or infrequently – doesn't hurt the people they're talking about. It hurts themselves. Deeply.

Why? Because trash gets spread, number one. In fact, there are lots of people in our personal and professional circles who love to spread the stuff we say around. Even the ones we truly believe will hold our stuff sacred might just go and gab about it.

The second thing is this. Talking trash makes you a *trash talker*. If you've done it once, you've done it twice... and you will become known for it. People won't trust you, won't go one level deeper with you (see Leadership Lesson #3). Perhaps worst of all, they'll respect you less.

Think about people you know who talk trash about their organizations, their bosses, their colleagues, their boards. Think of those who gossip, who judge others out loud to anyone who will listen.

It shouldn't be too hard to come up with some examples.

The truth is many of us don't just do it – we *love* to do it. When we talk about other people then we get to feel a bit better about ourselves by comparison. Which means we aren't as secure with ourselves as we like to pretend we are (see Leadership Lesson #7).

Even if we don't initiate it, we join in when others do. We figure it couldn't hurt. Not this one time.

But.

There are other people watching (see Leadership Lesson #5). They are listening. When they hear you lower your voice in a public place as you get ready to spread the dirt about your sister-in-law, they will listen harder. And if you're not doing it, but instead playing a passive role by listening and subsequently laughing a whole lot, you'll get the same reputation.

Trash talker.

Plus you'll fill your space with negative, toxic behavior. Not a great way to get your energy up and get things done (see Leadership Lesson #6)

I am constantly shocked at the amount, variety and depth of trash talking I see each day. People do it brazenly, talk about their boss in the middle of the lunchroom, about their terrible organizations right in the middle of a networking event. I've met people for the first time who feel okay trashing a mutual colleague when they have absolutely no clue how I feel about the person.

Whenever I see it or hear it, I take note. And I keep my own mouth shut.

Why? Because I clearly know that a person who talks trash about someone else will undoubtedly talk trash about me, too.

Now, think of the other people – the ones you can't crack. The ones who, even when you know things are tough back at the office, won't say a bad word about anything or anyone.

You might just hate that you can't get them to share some dirt. But chances are you also respect the heck out of them.

A brief example

I was on the buffet lunch line at a networking event and ran into a woman I'd met just once before. I noticed that her name badge reflected a new job at a new company.

Her response when I congratulated her?

"Thanks so much! Gosh, I'm so glad I got out of that other place. They just couldn't get their act together. This new organization is going to be wonderful now that they've

cleaned out some of their upper management."

I say it again. We'd met *once* before. And now here we stood, on a very long, *public* buffet line. In less than 30 seconds this woman had trashed not one, but two organizations - not to mention a whole lot of people inside each one.

I made a mental note. *Don't say anything. Don't join in. Don't trust any information.*

Steer clear.

Shortly afterwards I passed by her as she sat at a table of ten. She was giving the same speech. Loudly, and with more detail.

I couldn't help but wonder what they were all thinking.

I couldn't help but wonder how many joined in.

I couldn't help but wonder how many – as a result – hurt themselves right in that moment.

I wondered – but, trying to follow my own advice – I walked away before I could find out.

Today...

As tempting as it is, don't talk trash about anyone or anything or any place you are connected to, unless it is with your absolutely small core circle of trusted people, your SWAT team (see Leadership Lesson #5).

And when someone else starts talking trash to you, keep your mouth shut. Don't let yourself engage in the gossip. End it quickly.

You might just save your reputation.

LEADERSHIP LESSON #9
The Truth About Your Hunger

Perhaps you've noticed a trend when I talk about great leaders.

They tend to get under our skin.

They frustrate us because things seem to happen so easily for them.

They move up quickly in their companies. They secure bigger salaries. They learn a new skill and execute it the very next day as though they've always been a pro.

The rest of us stand by and watch and – let's be honest – get a bit huffy about it.

Why does life just seem to come so easily for some people? Why do others flock to them with such great opportunities? Why do they get to be so lucky when the rest of us have to muddle through the daily grind for so much longer – and why is our particular daily grind so much harder?

First of all, we all know the reality of the situation. Things actually don't come any easier for great leaders. They just make it look that way.

So what makes them so special? What's the difference? Just how do they make things happen for themselves? It's all about this next truth...

TRUTH #9
*Great Leaders Know
What They Want and
Go After it Relentlessly*

Simply put, great leaders are hungry.

They don't work in existing systems. They change the systems to give them what they want. They come up with new options for jobs, projects and professional development that their bosses hadn't even thought of. They see an opportunity coming their way before most of the rest of us have looked up from our laptops, and they seize it.

They convince others to let them try something new, move up before their resume says they should, take a risky new initiative. And they do it with confidence, with their fists pumped and a strong, knowing look in their eyes.

And they get what they want.

Their simple steps?

First, they know what they want. Unlike the rest of us.

All too often we settle into our daily machine without even thinking about it. We become "ants marching", making our way from one place to another by sheer habit, the way ants march from place to place in a single, straight line.

We sit in our office cubicle and pump out the same report and tell ourselves that this is the way things need to be right now. Our job is our job, our life is our life and we don't have much say in the matter unless we want to throw our world and our families into chaos.

We allow ourselves to believe that we don't have options, that we fit into this box that the world has created and we need to either stay or move on to something drastic. It's a comfortable place to be, settled into this belief.

It's also boring. And frustrating.

Great leaders know otherwise. They think differently.

Great leaders fill out a report once and realize it can be done more efficiently. So they change it.

Great leaders pass by a golf course and realize they want to give it a try. So they buy some clubs, take a few lessons, work hard at it, and out-par us all.

Great leaders look around them at their companies and check out what the cool guy next to them is doing, then figure out how to do something similar within their own jobs.

Great leaders pay attention to what gives them energy and expand on that (see Leadership Lesson #6). They watch what others are up to and say "I want to do that." Then they go after it.

And they're explicit. They tell those that have a say exactly what they want. They make a compelling case. They play those politics with those who can give it to them (see Leadership Lesson #1).

And, in the end, they get it all.
And they make it look easy.

A brief example...

I spent a brief bit of time working in broadcast news. I
began as an intern and moved my way up from there
– doing all kinds of menial and administrative tasks
until I began coordinating special projects, then taking on some writing for one of the newscasts. Each
time I moved up I did it the way everyone else did. I
waited for something to open up and applied for it. I
was young and new and figured I didn't have much of
a say in how my day-to-day shook out. Until I got put
on the assignment desk.

I hated the assignment desk.

The assignment desk is the center, the heart of the
newsroom. It's a buzzing hub of chaos, of stress, of loud
– often angry – voices. Voices of reporters and produc-
ers, photographers and managers, all wanting to have
their say in how things get done. And I was to manage
them all.

Ironically I was put on the desk as a promotion. It
was a more powerful position, came with more money.

The boss was excited to tell me that I'd made it there.

The problem was I knew I'd hate it. I knew I'd dread coming to work each day.

My end goal wasn't to work the desk. It was to produce the news.

I was so desperate that I took what I thought was a desperate risk. When I was told I would be working the desk, I responded with this:

"You know, the desk isn't my ultimate goal, but I know you need someone on it. What if I did the desk for four days each week, and on the fifth I shadowed a producer so I can learn how to help with that as well?"

The manager thought about it while I held my breath, wondering where that bit of fire came from.

"Deal," she said.

And so that's what happened. I came in at midnight for five Mondays in a row and observed the producer who put together the morning show. I worked the desk the rest of the week.

On the fifth Monday she told me she was leaving.

On the sixth Monday I was officially producing the show myself.

True story.

Today...

Think about what you want. Think differently about your options. Notice what gives you energy. Notice what others are doing that seems interesting.

Consider new jobs, new projects, new skills, new hobbies.

Then, get hungry. Be explicit.

Go after it. Relentlessly.

LEADERSHIP LESSON #10
The Truth About the Way You Communicate

I've saved one of my favorites for #10. Trust me, if you master this one, you stand way, way out.

A few questions before we begin.

How many people do you talk to each day? In person? By phone?

How many people email you, connect with you online?

They might all be different, but I'm willing to bet they almost all have a few things in common.

They write…fine. They speak…fine.

Chances are their messages are sprinkled with a few errors, their stories might be a bit longer than you need. Perhaps you get those emails that are just fragmented, super-short responses to your questions. No hello. No good-bye.

And chances are this is all fine with you. After all, we're all busy and dealing with dozens – if not hundreds – of people each day. Plus it gives us license to do the very same thing.

But…here's my last question.

How many of those dozens – if not hundreds – of conversations, emails and connections will you remember in a given day?

Not too many.

But I bet you remember the ones from great leaders, who embrace this next truth…

TRUTH #10

Great Leaders Insist On Excellent, Pristine Communication

Great leaders know that every interaction is an opportunity to connect with people in a way that is relatable and professional. To go a level deeper. To be memorable in some way. To *get* something - if not today, then perhaps tomorrow.

Every time they speak, every time they write, they do it with care. It's not obvious because they also do it with ease. But, I promise you, they think it through.

Their emails are neither three words nor 300. They begin with a mild pleasantry, say what they need to say in a carefully worded message, and end it in a friendly tone. They use as few words as possible to get the message across directly, professionally and with just enough personality to remind you why you like them so much.

I spend a lot of time on writing in *The Mission Myth*, where I also identify the biggest mistake we make when we do it: we fail to think like the person reading our stuff. Instead, we think only about how interesting we, ourselves, find our own material to be, and assume others will feel the same. But now we know they won't, because we know that nobody will find us as interesting as we do (see Leadership Lesson #3).

I work on this reality every day. In fact, I cut 100 pages from *The Mission Myth* before it went to print because I wanted to keep things moving for the reader. It's also the reason you've almost reached the end of this book even though it might feel like you just cracked it open.

Great leaders don't stop at great writing. Their in-person conversations provide just enough information about themselves to intrigue you, but always with a focus on turning it back to you. They don't ramble. They don't waste your time. Their conversations are focused and thought through – and they have an uncanny, intuitive ability to do it on the fly.

You won't experience many grammatical offenses in either their written or spoken words, or any kind of unpleasant tone. They spell check every single thing that goes out. They read it over quickly, just to be sure it's what they want. They check to make sure they've attached the correct document to every email before hitting *send*.

When you come across these people and their messages, you pay attention. You read their emails before others because you know they're worth your time. You talk to them more because you enjoy their company.

Many people – many perfectly good leaders in fact – feel that pristine communication is unnecessary. They believe people know who they are, that there is no need to treat every communication with such care. And it's probably true.

Great leaders, on the other hand, don't see these kinds of enhanced communication as a bother. Instead they see each one as an opportunity. To stand out. To go deeper. To get what they want.

And so they do.

A brief example...

My Dad was great at this.

Any conversation with him left you feeling like he cared about you – and only you – during the time you spent together. Any email from him came with a logical sequence, a warm but succinct opening, a warm but succinct close.

His goal with every correspondence was to impress upon you both that he cared and that he knew what he was doing. He didn't muck up his communication with lots of extra words and stories. And he punctuated his words with a smile and a laugh.

My Dad connected with people because he set out to connect with people. Every day. Every time. He didn't leave his interactions to chance. He inspired you with his words. Because he knew every one counted.

A consummate and lifelong salesman, my Dad was a genius at using the written and spoken word to stand out. When he was pitching and got the question about what he or his company accomplished, his words were always the same.

"Instead of telling you, why don't I show you?" And then he'd pull out a brief report, written out carefully beforehand, and he'd walk his customer through the results he'd accomplished. Then he'd tell them what he could accomplish for them as well. He then shook their hands heartily and walked out confidently, passing by the others who were waiting to go in and do their thing. And knowing that they wouldn't be as good as him.

The result? My Dad got sales. My Dad got promoted. My Dad was liked. My Dad was loved.

My Dad was successful in life.

My Dad was a great leader.

My Dad gave me something to strive for.

Today…

Practice making each conversation – written or in-person – excellent. Think through your words for just a second before you say them. Read your emails over before you send them. See them as an opportunity.

Over time it won't just become second nature. It will make you rise above the rest.

WRAPPING IT UP

So you made it...all the way through ten tough truths. Congratulations! I hereby give you a big, fat pat on the back.

Because, as tough as these truths might be, you've proven one thing.

You are, too.

You're tough because you care enough about being successful to read through a few unpleasant lessons and make it to the other side.

You're tough because you're willing to believe at least some of what you read here and even test yourself a bit to see if it works for you.

You're tough because you want to achieve the optimal level of greatness, and you're willing to take yourself out of your comfort zone to get there.

or this, I give you a lot of credit. Because I know you're going to go far.

Just remember the following to make it a bit easier...

• We're in this together. Many of us are still smack dab in the middle of the path to greatness. Welcome to the club.

• You don't have to focus on all of the truths all of the time. Pick your favorite or, better yet, pick the one you resist the most. There's a reason you don't like it, so you best start there.

• There are small things you can do every day that will make a significant difference in your success.

Let's review a few, shall we?

1. Practice politics. Work a relationship with everything you've got and see what happens as a result.

2. Know that being successful means not everyone will like you, but you're still a good person anyway. In fact, you're a great leader. So hold your head high no matter what others say, and focus on those who are on your side.

3. Remember that your stories are not as interesting to others as they are to you, so keep them short and compelling, then turn your focus to the other guy. Do it today.

4. Trust me that everyone is afraid. Resist letting yourself feel lesser than those who are successful because they appear to be fearless. They're not. They are just as scared as the rest of us. They just have the gumption to do the tough stuff anyway. Let yourself do the same.

5. Next time you are tempted to roll your eyes, huff and puff at a meeting or fidget at a networking event, resist. Someone's watching you.

6. Cut something out of your life that sucks the energy out of you. Add something in that boosts it. Both of these might very well be people.

7. Figure out where your greatest insecurities lie, what is keeping you from taking risks. Then do something to fix it, do something great, and give the credit to everyone else.

8. When you want to talk trash about someone today, resist with all your might. Then know you stand out from the pack.

9. Pay attention to something new that interests you or what you envy about the lives of others. Then take one aggressive step towards it.

10. Don't let one email go out or tell one story that isn't excellent in its grammar and content. Insist on perfection for one day and see how others pay attention.

Now, this list doesn't feel so bad, does it? In fact, I'm absolutely certain you can do at least one of these today.

So do it. Know that you're on your way to greatness.

Know that you're probably even closer than you think.

Know that you are tougher than any of these tough truths.

BONUS LEADERSHIP LESS...
The Truth About
Your Life

Yes, there's a bonus lesson.

I include it not to be clever. I include it because I think it's extremely important.

It comes back to one of my most important, and most humbling lessons. And at first blush it will seem so very obvious. But it's not.

Which is why I again ask you to stick with me.

So here it is. The final lesson I've learned from great leaders...

BONUS TRUTH
Great Leaders
Have a Life

I bring this truth up for different reasons than you might be thinking.

Sure, we all know the benefits of having a life. Of spending time with loved ones, taking trips, finding new hobbies.

We all know that it helps us create that ever-elusive "work-life balance". That it refreshes us, leaves us happier about coming to work the next day. Not to mention we won't get divorced or have our kids hate us because we're never around.

But there's another reason to have a life. And it's this.

When you have a life you remember something important. And, like the other lessons, it can even sting a bit.

When you have a life you realize that your life is not the sun. That you are not the center of all things important. That the lives of others don't revolve around you.

That the issues you're dealing with at your organization don't matter to most people.

That the challenges you face that feel so unique to you…aren't.

That the people around you who love you – or don't – don't hold all of the opinions of all the people in all of the world.

That your successes are great…but others have them, too.

That your failures hurt…but others have them, too.

When we make our whole lives entirely about our own work, we fall into the false idea that our work is all that matters. To anyone. To everyone.

We forget that millions of people every day have their own stuff going on. They don't care about anything we're dealing with.

And when we realize this – when we realize the successes and failures of the world actually don't rest on our very fine shoulders, those shoulders can't help but relax.

Great leaders have a life not just to get some time away.

They have a life to get perspective. To learn about the lives of others. To remember that they are not the most important people in the world, and the things they are tackling are not the most important things.

Embrace this truth. It might sting a bit at first, take a toll on the old ego.

But it will also let you breathe a bit easier.

Because you'll realize your life isn't the sun.

Which will ultimately make you better at it.

A brief example…

Back when I ran a nonprofit organization in Denver I played poker tournaments. There was a weekly game in particular that I never, ever missed.

It was on Tuesday evenings, and each week at 5:30pm found me changing out of my slacks and into my jeans right before racing around the back streets of the city to get a good parking spot and find the right seat.

Those watching as I breezed out of the office would turn to each other and say "Wow, Deirdre must *really* like poker."

And I did. But that's not why I went every single Tuesday.

I went to get a life. I needed to sit next to people who didn't give a care whether or not I made payroll, whether or not my staff liked me, whether or not we were meeting our strategic goals.

The importance of this came to me early, on a random Tuesday, when a random guy next to me made the mistake of asking me how I was doing.

Here's how it went:

Poker playing guy: Oh, hey Deirdre. Good to see you. Hey, how's it going?

Deirdre (breathlessly): It's okay. Though I'm pretty stressed because I'm waiting to hear back on a big grant

...or my organization, and if it doesn't come in I don't know how I'm going to make budget.

Poker playing guy: That's too bad. Hey, did that guy just show a pair of 8s over there?

I was stunned. Did he not see my torment, feel my pain?

Or...I realized, perhaps he just didn't care that much. Because my life really didn't impact him at all.

Because my life was not the sun.

It was a critical lesson. Nobody wanted to hear about my work, so I didn't have to talk about it. For just a few hours I could focus on other things, forget that work even existed, remember there's a life outside of it.

It turned out poker was great for me, and not because of the cards I was dealt at the table.

Because I could forget about the rest of the cards I was dealt in life.

Today...

Even in your most dire moments, even when it seems like the world will come crashing down around you, even when it seems like nobody likes you anymore... remember this.

It won't. And they do.

Because your life is not the sun.

Then get a life so you can remember it every single day.

ABOUT THE AUTHOR

The bad news for Deirdre Maloney is that she made a lot of mistakes. The good news is she worked really hard to make each one only once. With each error she figured out what went wrong, the part she played, and how to avoid it again.

This exact process is how Deirdre has become a nationally recognized speaker and author known for her personal brand of "mild audacity". She wrote her first book, *The Mission Myth*, after running a multi-million dollar nonprofit for nearly a decade and learning painful lessons along the way. The book explores her journey and uses validation, humor and concrete tips to help others avoid some of the same pain.

Deirdre figured out the *Tough Truths*, the topic of her second book, using the same non-scientific technique. In this case, however, things were a bit different. Even though she's figured out how the tough truths create great leaders, she finds she still needs to practice them daily. And sometimes she'll still mess them up. Because, in the end, that's part of the chess game called life.

When Deirdre's not writing or speaking she proudly runs Momentum LLC, which helps organizations exceed their goals and helps their leaders sleep better at night. She also teaches marketing for the University of San Diego's School of Leadership and Education Sciences and is known for her popular blog on all things leadership.

In her spare time Deirdre is a body-builder. She rises at 4:30 each morning to focus her energy on lifting weights, creating not just new levels of physical and mental strength, but also continued peace of mind.

Deirdre currently lives in San Diego with Jason, her beloved husband, travel buddy, IT guy, web designer, sushi-roll-splitter and high-shelf-reacher.

For more information on Deirdre, visit:
www.makemomentum.com